INTO THE WOODS
A WOODLAND SCRAPBOOK

Loretta Krupinski

HARPERCOLLINSPUBLISHERS

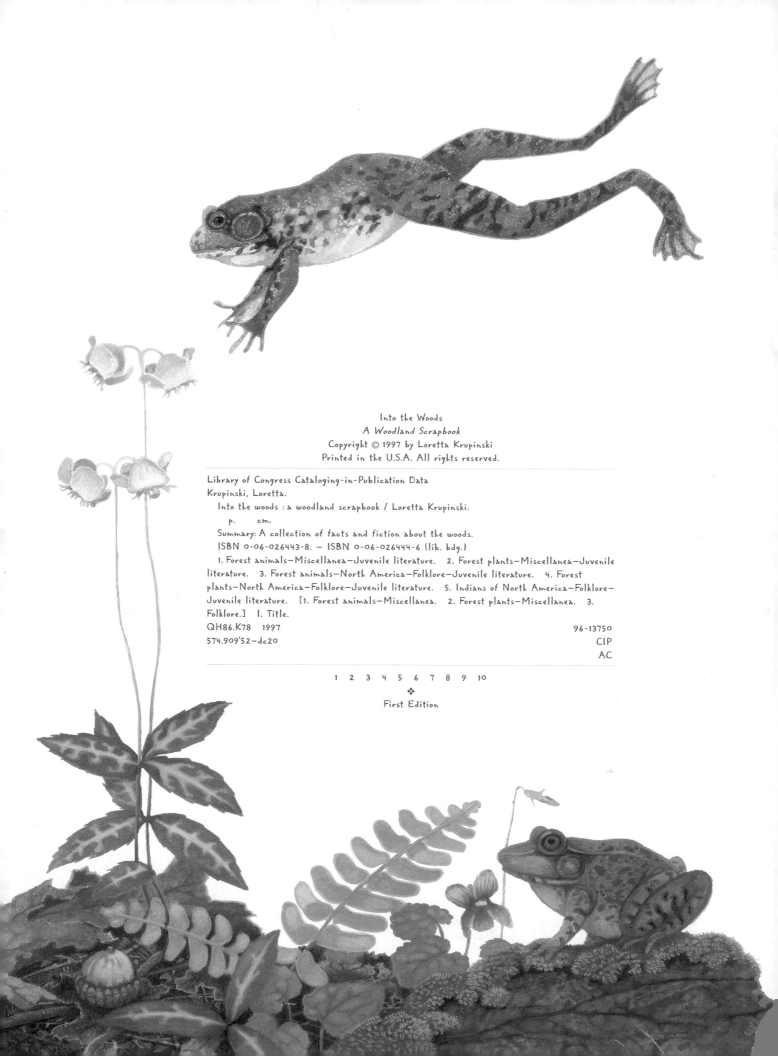

Into the Woods
A Woodland Scrapbook
Copyright © 1997 by Loretta Krupinski
Printed in the U.S.A. All rights reserved.

Library of Congress Cataloging-in-Publication Data
Krupinski, Loretta.
  Into the woods : a woodland scrapbook / Loretta Krupinski.
      p.   cm.
  Summary: A collection of facts and fiction about the woods.
  ISBN 0-06-026443-8. — ISBN 0-06-026444-6 (lib. bdg.)
  1. Forest animals—Miscellanea—Juvenile literature.   2. Forest plants—Miscellanea—Juvenile
literature.   3. Forest animals—North America—Folklore—Juvenile literature.   4. Forest
plants—North America—Folklore—Juvenile literature.   5. Indians of North America—Folklore—
Juvenile literature.   [1. Forest animals—Miscellanea.   2. Forest plants—Miscellanea.   3.
Folklore.]   I. Title.
QH86.K78   1997   96-13750
574.909'52—dc20   CIP
                                                                         AC

1 2 3 4 5 6 7 8 9 10
❖
First Edition

TREASURE HUNT

I found a door,
where pine and fallen branches
make a wall.
I push through,
to another world—
the sun is dim,
the wind is stopped.
Mushrooms poke through moss,
a bird's nest brushes my head.
Inside, three eggs
the size of my thumb!
A woodpecker drums,
a spider droops her swag
of silk, and I,
my treasure hunt complete,
go through the pine needle door,
back to fields and sun.

—Ann Turner

Deer

Only male deer have antlers. They shed their antlers every winter, and new ones grow in their place each spring.

A fawn's spots help to hide it from predators. The spots fade in the fall, when the fawn is three months old.

Chipmunks

The chipmunk stores seeds and nuts in a burrow in the ground for the winter months ahead. Chipmunks spend most of their day sleeping in underground burrows that can reach twelve feet in length. In the winter they plug up their burrow entrance and live off the food they've stored below.

The chipmunk stuffs seeds and nuts into its cheek pouches to hoard for the winter.

HOW THE CHIPMUNK GOT ITS STRIPES
AN IROQUOIS LEGEND

Long ago the Earth knew only darkness. One day the animals in the forest gathered together to decide if it would be better to remain in darkness or to bring in daylight. Deer, squirrels, raccoons, wolves, and many others climbed up to the top of a high mountain. The mountain stood so high that its bald face was covered with rocks and shrouded in stars and clouds.

The biggest and most powerful animal of all—the bear—stood at the peak and argued for darkness. Many animals agreed that they could sleep more in darkness, as there would be no light to keep them awake. The wolves said they could howl in darkness or in light. It was only the chipmunk who spoke for the light.

As they argued, the first sunrise ever to be seen sent its rays of light through the clouds and then across the rocks on the mountaintop. The chipmunk began to chatter and dance from rock to rock. The bear was so angry that he didn't get his way, he chased the chipmunk down the mountain. The chipmunk barely escaped with his life, but to this day you can see the stripes on his back where the bear scratched him with his claws.

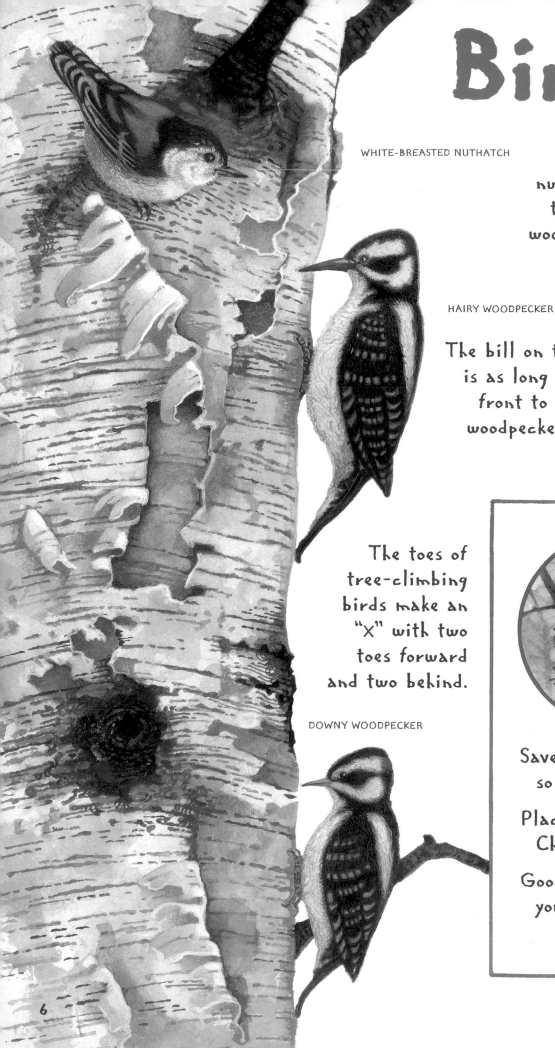

Birds

WHITE-BREASTED NUTHATCH

The white-breasted nuthatch walks down a tree headfirst, unlike woodpeckers, who climb down tail first.

HAIRY WOODPECKER

The bill on the hairy woodpecker is as long as its head from the front to the back. The downy woodpecker has a smaller bill.

The toes of tree-climbing birds make an "X" with two toes forward and two behind.

DOWNY WOODPECKER

Save a fallen nest, so tiny and dear.

Place it on your Christmas tree.

Good fortune will be yours for the year.

—Tradition

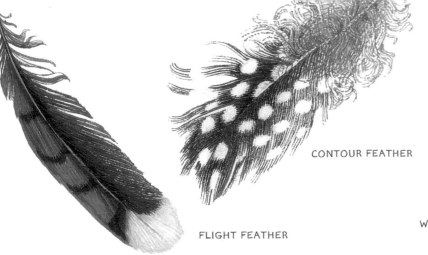

CONTOUR FEATHER

FLIGHT FEATHER

These winter birds either eat seeds or search the bark of trees for insects.

TUFTED TITMOUSE

WINTER WREN

PURPLE FINCH

CHICKADEE

A bird has different types of feathers. The stiff quills of the flight feather, found on the wings and tail, enable a bird to fly. Contour feathers protect the bird from harsh weather and keep it warm in winter.

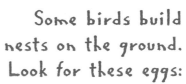

CONTOUR FEATHER

A white-throated sparrow has built a nest among the common blue violets.

Some birds build nests on the ground. Look for these eggs:

HERMIT THRUSH

OVENBIRD

SLATE-COLORED JUNCO

Animal Tracks

The red fox does not hibernate in winter. But when it naps, it curls into a ball and tucks its bushy tail over its nose like a blanket.

RED FOX

The deer mouse eats berries and seeds in winter.

DEER MOUSE

MOOSE

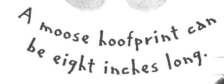

A moose hoofprint can be eight inches long.

In the woods of the northeastern and central United States only two animals have hooved tracks: the moose and the white-tailed deer.

The river otter's thick tail leaves a wide mark in the snow in between its paw prints.

RIVER OTTER

SNOWSHOE HARE

COTTONTAIL RABBIT

Cottontail rabbit tracks are smaller than those of the snowshoe hare.

COYOTE

DOG

FRONT PAW PRINT

Dogs leave a staggered track. Wild canines, such as coyotes, make tracks in a straight line.

A black bear's back paw print is nine inches long.

GRAY SQUIRREL

BACK PAW PRINT

TAIL TRACK

CHIPMUNK

MUSKRAT

Look for raccoon tracks in the mud along streambeds, where raccoons go to wash their food before they eat.

RACCOON

9

Woodlore

SIGNS IN STONE

THIS IS THE TRAIL.

TURN TO THE LEFT.

TURN TO THE RIGHT.

IMPORTANT WARNING

SIGNS IN GRASS

THIS IS THE TRAIL.

TURN TO THE RIGHT.

TURN TO THE LEFT.

IMPORTANT WARNING

Trail signs show the direction of the trail; you can read the signs left by a person you are following, and you can make these signs for those who come after you.

It's said that when the horns of a crescent moon point upward, the month will be dry, because the moon can hold water. But when the horns tilt or point down, the water can run out, so the month will be rainy.

Old, fallen pieces of birch bark and dried pine needles are quick-lighting tinder for starting campfires. Never burn hemlock wood in a campfire near a tent, because it throws out sparks.

When you face north, then south is behind you, east is on your right, and west is on your left.

Look for the Big Dipper. If you extend an imaginary line from the bottom of the bowl, it will lead to the North Star. The Big Dipper circles around the North Star during the year, but the North Star is constant; so you will always be able to find north in a clear night sky.

GREAT HORNED OWL

The oil from the three-leaved poison ivy vine causes severe rashes and itching. When in doubt, don't touch!

POISON IVY

Nighttime in the woods is the time to hear owls, because they sleep all day and hunt all night. Their calls vary from a hair-raising screech (screech owl) to the "hoo, hoo-hoo, hoo, hoo" of the great horned owl.

Mushrooms

BLEWIT

CHANTERELLE

SHORT-STALKED
WHITE *RUSSULA*

PARASOL MUSHROOM

Mushrooms cannot make their own food the way green plants can. A mushroom is made up of thousands of fine threads that reach into the earth or into dead wood to find food and water. The mushroom makes spores instead of seeds. Spores grow into new mushroom threads.

"Toadstool" is an old name for a poisonous mushroom. Identifying mushrooms is tricky, so it's best not to eat any you find in the woods.

FLY AGARIC

BLUSHER

FLAT-TOPPED AGARICUS

If you step on a puffball, it explodes with a pop and squirts out a powdery dust cloud of spores.

PUFFBALL

Bracket fungi live on live or dead trees. They are hard and look like shelves.

RUSTY-GILLED POLYPORE

Fairy rings grow in circles. The underground threads of the mushrooms continue to spread out in search of food, which causes the ring to widen each year. Legend tells that the rings mark where fairies danced on moonlit nights.

CHRISTMAS FERN

Turkey-tail looks like fanned-out turkey-tail feathers. It grows mostly on dead oaks and maples.

TURKEY-TAIL

Rabbits

RABBIT AND THE BRIER BUSH
A FOLKTALE

Long ago, wild roses grew in clusters on bushes that had no thorns. However, squirrels and mice would climb up to eat the blossoms; moose would knock them over with their horns; possums would twitch them off with their tails; and deer would crush them with their hooves.

So the brier rose grew thorns to protect its delicate flowers from all these animals. Only the cottontail rabbit remained its friend. The rabbit does not climb, doesn't have horns or hooves, and has only a tiny, fluffy tail.

And that is why now when a rabbit is in danger, he seeks safety from the brier bush, who defends him with thousands of tiny dagger-shaped thorns.

Before getting out of bed on the first day of each month, say, "Rabbit, rabbit." Some people believe this will bring you good luck for the rest of the month.

SNOWSHOE HARE

In summer the fur of the snowshoe hare changes from white to brown.

Cottontail rabbits have shorter hind feet than the snowshoe hare. In winter they munch on twigs and the lower branches of evergreens.

EASTERN COTTONTAIL RABBIT

Coyotes

Coyotes are seen from dawn to dusk, and they like to howl at night. Unlike wolves, which live in packs, coyotes tend to live on their own.

SENSITIVE FERNS

BUTTERCUPS

Raccoons

Raccoons live near water. They like to eat frogs, clams, and crayfish, and any leftovers they might find in garbage cans. They raise their families in hollow trees. Raccoons are nocturnal animals; they are only active at night.

MARSH MARIGOLDS

Wildflowers

"Jack" is inside the striped hood ("pulpit"), which varies in color from green to purple. In fall red fruits found inside are eaten by ring-necked pheasants and wild turkeys.

TRAILING ARBUTUS

JACK-IN-THE-PULPIT

After their first long winter in America, the Pilgrims discovered this flower. It gave them new hope. They called it "mayflower."

WINTERGREEN

Wintergreen's crushed leaves smell like candy. Yum!

PARTRIDGE-BERRIES

Red partridgeberries are eaten by mice, chipmunks, and grouse. The twin berries are joined in the middle.

INDIAN PIPES

Indian pipes are shaped like a cluster of clay pipes. As they age, the nodding flowers turn upward and change from white to brown. Because the plant lacks chlorophyll, it cannot produce its own food, so it takes nutrients from decaying plant matter (as mushrooms do).

Jewelweed dangles like an earring. Its crushed stems and leaves can be used to relieve the itch of poison ivy.

JEWELWEED

Hepatica flowers and spring azure butterflies are among the earliest signs of spring. They appear even when snow is still on the ground. Bees also awake from their deep winter sleep at this time.

Bloodroot blooms in the spring. Native Americans used the red-colored sap from the roots as a dye for clothing and baskets, as ceremonial body paint, and as medicine.

SPRING AZURE BUTTERFLY

GOLDEN NORTHERN BUMBLEBEE

HEPATICA

BLOODROOT

Maples

Among the most colorful trees in autumn are the maples. Cool nights and bright sunshine bring out the best fall colors. Too much rain makes the colors dull.

SUGAR MAPLE

SAP BUCKETS

SILVER MAPLE WITH
WINGED SEEDS

The Native Americans taught early settlers how to tap maple trees and boil the sap to make syrup. Mild days and below-freezing nights from January through April make the sap rise. Buckets hung from spouts collect the sap. It takes 35 gallons of sap to make 1 gallon of maple syrup.

Birches

GRAY BIRCH

WHITE BIRCH

White and gray birches have white peeling bark.
If you remove the bark, it never grows white again.

WHITE BIRCH

Sassafras

Sassafras tea can be made by boiling the sweet, fragrant roots of the young trees. The colonists traded sassafras to England, where it was used to cure illnesses such as colds and stomachaches.

The sassafras tree has leaves of three different shapes. One is shaped like a mitten.

THE BEAVER AND THE PORCUPINE
A HAIDA LEGEND

Porcupine was lazy, but he was also hungry. One day he decided to steal food from Beaver, since they both liked to eat bark from the same trees. Beaver was furious and started a fight with Porcupine, during which he received a faceful of sharp porcupine quills.

Beaver called on his family for help. The beaver clan carried Porcupine to a remote island where there were no trees that Porcupine could eat. Fearing death, Porcupine began to sing songs of the north. Soon the North Wind began to blow, and the weather became so cold that the water around the island turned to ice. Porcupine escaped.

Then Porcupine sought revenge. He and his family carried Beaver to the top of the tallest tree in the forest and left him there to die, since beavers cannot climb trees. However, Beaver simply ate the tree from the top down to the bottom until he reached the ground.

Porcupine no longer steals food, and Beaver avoids Porcupine and his sharp quills.

Porcupines

Baby porcupines are called porcupettes. Porcupines defend themselves by swinging their tails or lunging at their enemies in order to embed their sharp quills. They do not eject the quills.

Patches of gnawed bark high up on tree trunks and branches tell us porcupines are living there. They are tree dwellers.

Beavers

Beavers cut down twigs, saplings, and small branches to make a lodge, where the family lives. The beaver lodge is part of the dam, which causes a stream to flood and form a pond. The lodge usually has two underwater entrances.

It takes two days for a beaver to cut down a tree. It eats only the bark, but it chews on the wood to keep its teeth worn down; otherwise its teeth would grow so long that it couldn't eat.

Seeds

TULIP TREE

AMERICAN BASSWOOD

RED MAPLE

Plants grow in new places every year because their seeds are scattered by animals, humans, and even the weather.

These seeds have wings and are scattered by the wind.

ALDER

The alder's flowery catkins become seed-bearing cones.

DOGWOOD

Berries

MAPLE-LEAVED VIBURNUM

Dogwood berries are eaten by birds and squirrels.

Nuts

Only some kinds of hickory nuts are edible. Nuts can be gathered in late fall. The husks split into four sections.

The large green husks of black walnuts are easy to spot. They look like tennis balls hanging in the branches.

BLACK WALNUT

WILD TURKEY

BEECH

Wild turkeys, raccoons, and bears like to eat acorns, hickory nuts, and beechnuts.

Conifers

Conifers are trees with needlelike or scaly leaves. The needles stay on the trees year round, so they are known as evergreens. Most conifers produce seeds in cones.

BALSAM FIR

The cones on fir trees sit upright on the branches. On spruce trees they hang down. The scales on the fir seed cones fall apart, leaving a long needle-shaped core. The fir is a popular choice for Christmas trees.

WHITE PINE CONE
4"–8"

Eastern hemlock needles grow flat on arching boughs and are whitish underneath. Cones are small, growing no larger than an inch.

EASTERN HEMLOCK

EASTERN RED CEDAR

Eastern red cedar, also called juniper, produces a blue berry instead of a cone. The scaly needles are four-sided, unlike those of the white cedar, whose needles are flat. This fragrant wood is deep red. Pencils used to be made from this wood.

A spruce needle is square like a wooden match, and the underside is not whitish, as it is in the hemlock and fir trees. Red spruce cones fall to the ground. They have a reddish color. Black spruce cones stay on the tree and lose scales one at a time. They are the smallest of the spruce cones.

BLACK SPRUCE

RED SPRUCE CONES

Pine needles are much longer than fir and spruce needles. White pine needles grow in clusters of five.

CARDINAL

WHITE PINE

Weather Lore

SPRING PEEPER

When spring arrives, the evenings are filled with the sounds of tiny frogs. A frog with an "X" mark on its back is a spring peeper. When the spring peeper sings, he inflates a large white bubble of skin under his mouth.

KATYDID

Legend says there will be a frost three months after the first katydid is heard.

RED-WINGED BLACKBIRD

AMERICAN ROBIN

Count the stars inside the halo or ring around the moon. Some say each star stands for the number of days before the weather will change again. Others say the stars stand for the number of bad-weather days to come.

The return of robins and red-winged blackbirds is a sign that spring is on its way.

V-shaped flocks of honking geese are often heard before they are spotted in the autumn sky. The geese migrate from cold northern areas to warmer areas in the south.

CANADA GOOSE

When the woolly bear caterpillar is more black than brown, the winter will be worse. However, brown at both ends means a mild winter.

WOOLLY BEAR CATERPILLAR

HOW GLOOSKAP CAPTURED SUMMER
AN ALGONQUIN LEGEND

Glooskap is a mythical figure who was responsible for the creation of the world, man and beast, and all inner goodness.

Glooskap headed north to go hunting. After a while he grew tired and cold. About this time he spotted the wigwam of a great giant named Winter. Winter gave him shelter and entertained him with stories, all the while casting a spell over Glooskap.

Glooskap slept for six months, and when he awoke, he left for his home in the south. On the way he came to a forest, green with leaves and ferns. In among the flowers little people were dancing. Their tiny queen was called Summer. Glooskap scooped her up in his hand and placed her in his pocket. Once more he journeyed north to the giant's wigwam. Now he would get even with Winter for making him sleep for six months.

Once again Winter tried to cast the spell of a deep, cold sleep. But the tiny queen hidden in Glooskap's pocket began to cast her powerful spell of warmth and growth. Soon Winter began to sweat, and eventually he and his wigwam melted away. Slowly, green leaves and grass began to grow. Birds began to sing. Glooskap placed Summer in a tiny birch bark canoe and sent her down the river, back to her kingdom of little people.

Then Glooskap made new arrows and a bow and went hunting, which is what he had set out to do in the first place.

Amphibians

Most amphibians hatch, and then spend the early part of their lives, in water. Later they develop lungs and live on land. They have moist, smooth skin. Both reptiles and amphibians are cold-blooded, which means their body temperature is regulated by their surroundings.

SPOTTED SALAMANDER

RED EFT

The red eft (eastern newt) changes to olive green with red spots in its land-dwelling stage.

The bullfrog is the largest and loudest frog. It grows up to eight inches in length.

BULLFROG

Frogs have smooth skin. They lay their eggs in clumps in the water. Toads feed on insects. Their eggs form long, jellied strings. Toads might look like they have warts. Contrary to what some people say, you can't get warts from touching a toad.

GREEN FROG

AMERICAN TOAD

Reptiles

Most reptiles live on land and have thick, scaly skin or plates.

The shape of a snake's head is sometimes used to identify whether it is poisonous or not. Most poisonous snakes have cheek pouches, giving them triangle-shaped heads. Most nonpoisonous snakes, however, have rounded heads, shaped like the end of your thumb.

EASTERN GARTER SNAKE (NONPOISONOUS)

TIMBER
RATTLESNAKE
(POISONOUS)

The eastern box turtle prefers damp woods. By drawing its head and legs into its squared-off shell, it seems to form a box.

EASTERN BOX TURTLE

EASTERN
PAINTED
TURTLE

The painted turtle lives in shallow freshwater streams and ponds.

RATTLES

BUNCHBERRY PLANTS

Squirrels

A red squirrel is half the size of a gray squirrel. It is most at home in coniferous forests, because it likes to eat the seeds it finds in pinecones. You might find its hidden pile of unopened seed cones in a hollow tree or in a hole in the ground.

The gray squirrel lives in oak or beech woods. In winter it uses its memory and sense of smell to dig up the acorns it buried in the fall. You might see its large nest of leaves in the bare tree branches in winter, though it might choose a tree hole for a nest instead.

Lichens are the slowest-growing of all plants.

CRUSTOSE LICHEN

BRITISH SOLDIER LICHEN

Oaks

Mighty oaks from little acorns grow.
—Proverb

RED OAK

There are two main groups of oaks. White oaks have rounded leaves, while red oaks have pointed leaves.

WHITE OAK

BLUE JAY   TUFTED TITMOUSE

Red oak acorns are bitter tasting. Most animals prefer to eat the sweeter white oak acorns, leaving the less popular red oaks to grow into new forests. Red oak trees outnumber white oaks for this reason.

Bears, deer, raccoons, and squirrels like to eat acorns. Many birds also like the tasty nut inside the shell.

SCARLET OAK   BLACK OAK   WHITE OAK   RED OAK   CHINQUAPIN

White oak acorns ripen in one year. Red oak acorns ripen in two years.

American Indians made flour from acorns by soaking them in a stream, drying them in the sunshine, and then pounding them into a powder.

Index

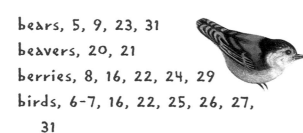
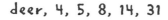
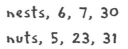
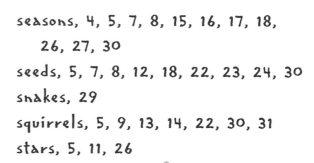